Simply Awesome Trips
Itineraries Ready To Go!

www.simplyawesometrips.com

Simply Awesome Trips offers personally experienced, detailed family trip itineraries to cities and outdoor destinations in the U.S. and abroad. Our goal is to help simplify your trip planning by sharing all the details you need for an enjoyable family vacation.

Each itinerary offers favorite lodging (including Airbnb and VRBO), local food recommendations, activities that were fun for both kids and adults, labeled maps, rainy day activities, and any helpful trip tips discovered along the way--all organized into detailed, day-by-day plans.

We've put in the hours to research a fantastic trip, our own families have loved them, and we provide all you need to experience the same. You can duplicate the trip in its entirety or gather ideas for your own itinerary. Have fun, be safe, and enjoy your time in Sedona and the Grand Canyon!

Happy Trails!

Amy & Amanda

Table of Contents

Introduction

Sedona, AZ is one of the most beautiful places I've experienced. The glow of the red rocks at sunset, the easy accessibility of fantastic hiking and biking trails, petroglyphs, ancient Indian cliff dwellings, and the nice weather make this a great family destination.

You're surrounded by 1.8 million acres of national forest land, yet you're never far from the town's shops, art galleries, and restaurants.

Sedona is within a 2 hour drive of Phoenix and roughly two hours from Grand Canyon National Park. The best time to visit Sedona is from March to May before it gets too blazing hot. September to November is also mild.

Getting There

Fly into Sky Harbor International Airport in Phoenix, AZ and drive 1:45 minutes north or fly into Flagstaff, AZ and drive 48 minutes south.

If you have a late arrival time in Phoenix and plan to drive to Sedona the next day, consider staying overnight at the **Scott Resort and Spa** in Scottsdale. We stayed there and loved their pool, and the rooms were nice as well.

Trip Overview

This is a one week itinerary with 3-4 nights in Sedona and 1-2 nights at the Grand Canyon National Park.

The last leg of this itinerary takes you on a scenic drive to the Grand Canyon with stops along the way at Sunset Crater National Monument and Wupatki National Indian Site. Recommendations for lodging, dining, and activities while visiting the Grand Canyon National Park are also included.

View from Boynton Canyon Trail in Sedona

Day	Morning	Afternoon
1	You've Arrived! Montezuma Castle National Monument (if time)	Check-in to lodging
2, 3, 4	Hike and enjoy the scenery in Sedona <u>Best Family Hiking Choices</u> •Bell Rock Hike •Baldwin Trail •Fay Canyon •V Bar V Heritage Site •Boynton Canyon Trail	Pool time during the peak heat hours
5	Drive to Grand Canyon National Park See Sunset Crater Volcanic National Monument and Wupatki National Monument on the way	Grand Canyon National Park Desert View Watch Tower Check-in to lodging
6	Bike the South Rim Walk the Rim Trail	Attend a Ranger Program
7	Return to Phoenix for your flight home (3.5 hour drive from Grand Canyon to Phoenix Sky Harbor Airport)	Stay overnight in Scottsdale if needed

Where to Stay

Sedona is known for its traffic during weekends and peak season. You can avoid much of this congestion by staying in the **Village of Oak Creek** just 15 minutes south of Sedona proper. This area provides excellent access to trails, shops, and restaurants. It is also home to Red Rock Cafe which is an excellent "go to" restaurant for breakfast and lunch.

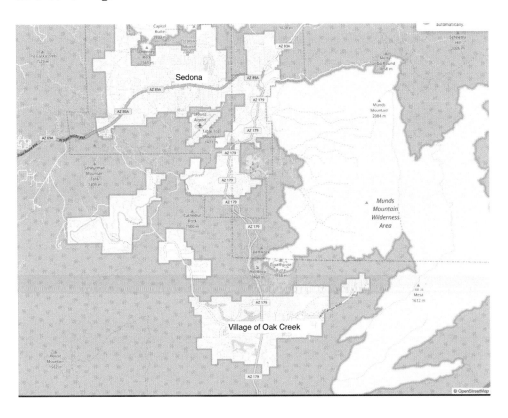

This is our personal list of places that we have stayed in previously, have been recommended by friends we trust, or we have bookmarked as possibilities for future visits. Determine your budget and you'll find plenty of options in this area.

Hilton Sedona Resort

Stay at the Hilton Sedona Resort in a one bedroom suite with a pullout sofa for the kiddos. Rooms come with a refrigerator, and the setting is beautiful. We would return in a heartbeat. It has beautiful views, a fantastic swimming pool which we enjoyed every afternoon, and a restaurant if you're too tired to go out. Average nightly price $280.

VRBO Properties

If you need more room, these nearby vacation properties look nice and are well located in the Village of Oak Creek.

1) 3 bedroom home, quiet, nice patio. No pool. Averaged $235 night. www.vrbo.com/3915247ha

2) 2 bedroom condo located next to the Hilton Sedona in the Ridge Resort. Has a nice pool. Averaged $344 night. www.vrbo.com/7090540ha

3) 1 bedroom condo with sleeper sofa located next to the Hilton Sedona in the Ridge Resort. Has a nice pool. Averaged $170 night. www.vrbo.com/847592vb

4) Nice 2 bedroom townhome, 1 King, 2 twins, sofa bed, sleeps 6. No pool access. Averaged $200 a night. https://www.vrbo.com/3967112ha

Day 1

You've Arrived! Visit Montezuma Castle on your way to Sedona.

Montezuma Castle National Monument

After picking up your rental car in Phoenix, head north towards Sedona. If driving from Phoenix to Sedona, plan on a little less than a 2 hour drive. If you have time, stop at Montezuma Castle National Monument, one of the best preserved cliff dwellings in North America. If you don't have time on the way, we would still make this a place to visit during your stay. Allow about 1 hour.

It is located 30 minutes from the Hilton Sedona and is an amazing preservation of ancient cliff dwellings. An easy walking tour provides the history while you gaze upon the ruins. Costs $10 per person; kids 15 and under are free. Admission is free with the America the Beautiful National Parks Pass.

Montezuma Castle- Photo courtesy of NPS

Days 2-4

Morning hikes and afternoon pool time

Overview

The best way to experience the scenery of Sedona's red rock formations is to explore this fantastic landscape on its trails. Sedona offers trails for any hiking level, and all of the hikes in this itinerary are suitable for a fun family outing. The trails described here are short and relatively easy with amazing scenic views with just a small investment of time and effort.

A typical day might include at least one hike in the morning before it gets too hot, and afternoon time relaxing at the hotel pool.

Remember to apply sunscreen, wear sturdy shoes, and bring plenty of water.

Red Rock Passes (Parking Passes)

This was a bit confusing to us at first, but it's actually pretty straight forward. Many of the hikes in the national forest require a "Red Rock Pass" to be displayed in your car when you park at the trailheads.

You will need a pass for most of my recommended hikes. If you have an America the Beautiful National Parks Pass ($80), you can display it instead of a Red Rock Pass. Otherwise, you will need to purchase a weekly ($15) Red Rock Pass or a Daily Pass ($5).

Red Rock Passes are available for sale at most of the Visitor Centers and is also sold at many grocery stores, gas stations, retail stores, and resorts. They are also offered at many of the trailheads. You can even purchase online- www.fs.usda.gov.

Tip: Consider buying the America the Beautiful National Park Pass. Not only will it grant you admission to other sites you'll be visiting on this trip (Montezuma Castle, Sunset Crater National Monument, Wupatki National Monument, and the Grand Canyon National Park) but you'll have admission to other national parks throughout the country for one year from date of purchase.

Favorite Hikes

These hikes are rated easy and suitable for most families. All provide an easy and short walk to incredible vistas. If you'd like a longer hike, these hikes have both short and longer options. Something for everyone!

Remember to bring your Red Rock Pass, plenty of water, and hike in the cooler part of the day if at all possible.

Hike	Round Trip Distance	Description
Bell Rock*	Approximately 1.5 miles or 3.6 mile option	Scramble up the most recognizable rock formation in Sedona for fantastic views and the chance to experience the vortex energy.
Baldwin Trail*	1 mile or 3.3 mile option	Enjoy iconic views of Cathedral Rock and stacking "buddahs" in the cool water of Oak Creek.
V Bar V Heritage Site	1/2 mile walk	Not really a hike per se, but an extraordinary opportunity to see one of the largest and best preserved petroglyph sites in the Verde Valley.
Boynton Canyon/ Boynton Vista Trail	1.2 miles or 6 mile option	Incredible views and the opportunity to scramble the large red rocks to two known vortex points.
Fay Canyon Trail*	1.5 miles or 3.5 mile option	Lovely hike to a natural stone arch with good views.

*If you only have time for a few hikes, Bell Rock, Baldwin Trail, and Fay Canyon are "must do" hikes. Because of the short length of these hikes, you could hike more than one in a day.

Bell Rock would be a good one to combine with another hike as it is the closest to the Village of Oak Creek and you can make it as short or long a hike (scramble) as you'd like.

Note: Fay Canyon and Boynton Canyon trailheads are closest to Sedona and furthest from the Village of Oak Creek- each about a 35 minute drive from the Hilton Sedona in the Village of Oak Creek.

What is a Vortex?

A vortex, as described to me, is a swirling concentration of energy emanating from the earth that can affect the human consciousness and even one's physical body. Many people have reported feeling inspired by these beneficial spiritual energy sources, which are also said to facilitate balance, prayer, healing, and intuitiveness. The Bell Rock vortex is best known for serenity and solving problems from a higher (spiritual) perspective. See if you feel it!

Map Overview of Trails

These maps show general trailhead locations and are courtesy of a partnership between the US Forest Service, Sedona Friends of the Forest, and a Keen Effect grant.

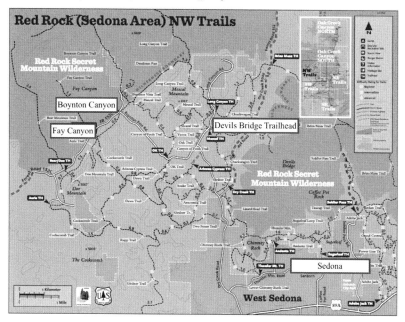

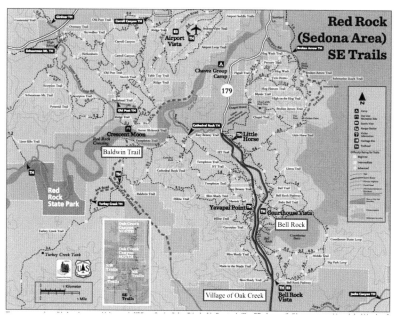

Note: V Bar V Heritage Site is south of the Village of Oak Creek.

Bell Rock Hike

Bell Rock is an iconic red rock formation located just north of the Village of Oak Creek and is an easy one to spot. My daughters loved hiking and climbing about half way up Bell Rock to the "meditation perch." Bell Rock is one of the most prominent Sedona vortex sites.

The unmistakable Bell Rock from afar

This is a moderate hike and will require supervision. It's roughly 1.5 miles round trip depending on how much "bouldering" you do. The views are beautiful and it's a fun scramble. Keep in mind, that you don't necessarily need an end point on this hike. You can climb to any point that is safe and affords a great view.

View from Meditation Perch

You can do as much or as little hiking as you'd like here- it's a fun place to hang out. Make sure you park in the *north* Bell Rock parking area (Courthouse Vista Parking Area)--the south side of Bell Rock is too steep to climb.

Once you park in the north lot, hike past the sign board and head to Bell Rock Trail. Follow it about 1/10th of a mile to its intersection with Courthouse Butte Loop Trail.

You can either continue on Bell Rock Trail to explore the northeast area of Bell Rock or turn right and follow Courthouse Butte Loop for approximately 500 feet to a sign post on your left. Turn left here and begin climbing up towards Bell Rock. Be sure to count the rock cairns and between the 10th and 11th cairn turn right and head towards the large flat rock shelf. You will see where you start to climb to Meditation Perch.

Want a longer hike?

If you don't want to scramble up Bell Rock or want to add more hiking distance, you can also walk the trail circling Bell Rock and Courthouse Butte. The Bell Rock Pathway is an easy, wide and flat trail totaling 3.6 miles roundtrip. There is a popular observation area on the west side of Bell Rock not accessible from the highway. Hiking it in a clockwise direction is recommended.

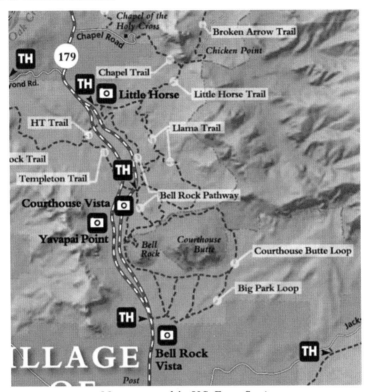

Map courtesy of the U.S. Forest Service

Directions to the <u>North</u> Trailhead--Courthouse Vista Trailhead (north of Bell Rock): From the Village of Oak Creek, take 179 north and turn right toward Courthouse Vista, milepost 308.2. Remember to display your Red Rock Pass.

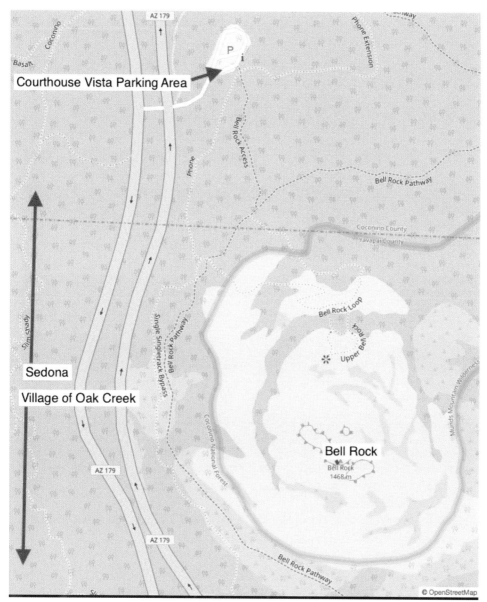

Bell Rock Trail: Park in the Courthouse Vista Parking Area

Baldwin Trail

This is another easy hike that you can make shorter or longer. You can hike the 3.3 mile Baldwin Loop Trail or simply take a short hike (roughly 1 mile) to the banks of Oak Creek with views of Cathedral Rock. It is simply a gorgeous setting. Cathedral Rock reflected in the waters of Oak Creek at Red Rock Crossing is one of the most photographed scenes in the southwest.

We hiked the loop trail with its magnificent red rock views and picnicked at Oak Creek. It's very close to the Sedona Hilton, so we returned several times to Oak Creek to build "buddahs" and play in the creek.

Oak Creek and Cathedral Rock

Hike the loop trail *clockwise* and within roughly 1/2 mile you will reach its intersection with the **Templeton trail** which takes you along the banks of Oak Creek. "Social trails" will also take you to Oak Creek. My girls enjoyed seeing dozens of "buddahs" where visitors have stacked small river rock into beautiful stone pillars. Return the way you came to the trailhead for a shorter hike or return to the Baldwin Trail to continue the loop.

Tip: Photos of Cathedral Rock are best taken during the afternoon, but you'll have to consider the heat of the day for the best time for your hike.

Directions: From the Village of Oak Creek, turn left on Verde Valley School Road and follow it to the end, roughly 4.5 miles. It will turn into a gravel road but is completely passable. Parking area is on the left. It's roughly 13 minutes from the Hilton Sedona. Remember to display your Red Rock Pass.

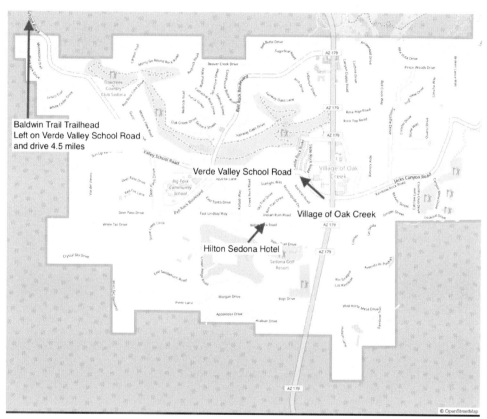

Follow Verde Valley School Road to reach the Baldwin Trail

V Bar V Heritage Site

The V Bar V Heritage Site is the largest known and best preserved petroglyph site in the Verde Valley.

Important: *It is only open on Friday, Saturday, Sunday, and Monday from 9:30 to 3pm.*

Although not really considered a hike, it does require a short 0.5 mile walk from the parking lot on the flat, maintained trail from the Visitor Center to the petroglyph area. The volunteers on site are extremely knowledgeable, very friendly, and obviously passionate about what they do.

Directions: V Bar V Heritage Site is located 2.8 miles east of the junction of I-17 and SR 179 on FR 618. Watch for the entrance on your right less than one-half mile past the Beaver Creek Campground.

It's a 15 minute drive south from the Hilton Sedona. Remember to display your Red Rock Pass.

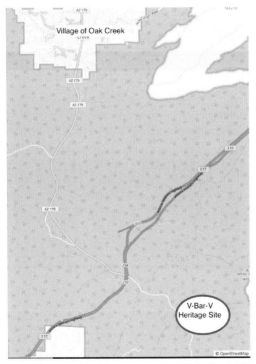

Wonderful petroglyphs 15 minutes south of Oak Creek Village

Petroglyphs at the V Bar V Heritage Site

Boynton Canyon Trail/Boynton Vista Trail

Boynton Canyon Trail View

The Boynton Canyon Trail is a 6 mile roundtrip hike. However, it is also the trailhead for a shorter (roughly 1.2 miles roundtrip), easier hike on the **Boynton Vista Trail**.

From the Boynton Canyon Trailhead, walk about 0.5 miles to its intersection with Boynton Vista Trail on the right. Follow it uphill to its two rock formations, both of which are considered vortex points. You'll find beautiful views, and my girls loved scrambling up the rocks. Bring your camera!

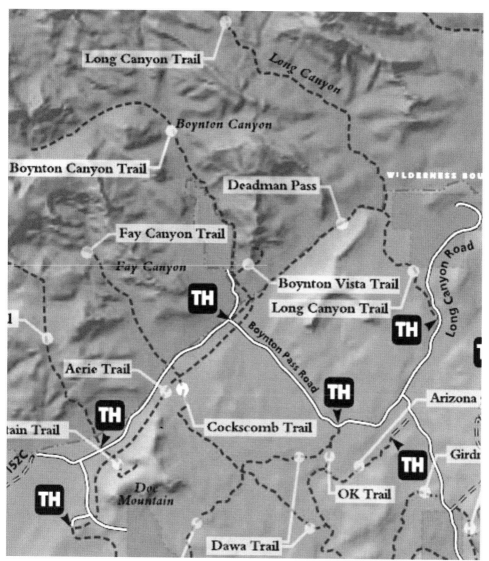

Map courtesy of the U.S. Forest Service

Rock climbing on the Boynton Vista Trail

Directions: From the Village of Oak Creek, drive 179 north to 89A continuing toward the west end of town. Turn north (right) on Dry Creek Road. Dry Creek Road ends at a " T " intersection. Follow the signs to Boynton Canyon.

You'll find a parking lot and the trailhead just outside the entrance to the Enchantment Resort. Closer to Sedona, it's about a 32 minute drive from the Hilton Sedona in the Village of Oak Creek. Remember to display your Red Rock Pass.

Fay Canyon Hike

This is another good hike with options for a short out and back or a longer 3.5 roundtrip hike. This easy hike through a canyon has wonderful views and intersects with a spur trail that leads to a natural stone arch and a narrow slot where the rocks have separated. The kids will have fun "disappearing" into the opening and enjoying the shade under the rock arch.

Arch Spur Trail: At about the 1/2 mile mark from the trailhead, look for a side trail up to the arch--it's easy to miss. You will have to scramble up a steep hill to see the arch (it's not visible from the main trail).

We returned to the trailhead from the arch for an out and back hike of roughly 1.5 miles, but you could return to the original main trail and continue on for views of Bear Mountain for a total of about 3.5 miles including the spur trail to the arch.

Fay Canyon Trail at the Arch

A nice rest in the shade of the arch

Directions: From the Village of Oak Creek, drive north on 179 to 89A through Sedona to Dry Creek Road (152C) at the west end of town. Turn right and follow Dry Creek Road three miles to the Boynton Canyon intersection then turn left. Go about a half mile to the Fay Canyon parking area on the left. Cross the street to the trailhead. It's about a 32 minute drive from the Hilton Sedona.

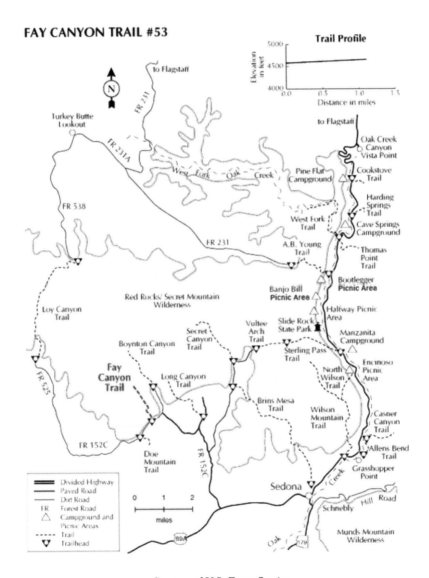

Courtesy of U.S. Forest Service

Additional Hikes

If you have time (unfortunately we did not), these hikes were also on my list though note that they are rated "moderate" rather than "easy." Apparently, everyone loves Devil's Bridge, and the Chapel of the Holy Cross looks like it would be a terrific destination hike.

- **Little Horse Trail/Chapel of the Holy Cross** - 4 miles roundtrip; moderate; beautiful hike to the Chapel of the Holy Cross, a church built into the rocks with spectacular views and peaceful atmosphere.

- **Devil's Bridge** - 2 miles roundtrip; moderate; the photos are super Instagram-worthy! Keep the kids close on this one.

Devil's Bridge

- **Brin's Mesa** - 4.4 miles roundtrip; moderate; the views on this hike apparently have a high "wow" factor. You'll gain 500 feet to a mesa overlooking Mormon Canyon and Soldiers Pass.

Hiking Resources

The Hike House, 431 State Route 179, is a great outdoors shop and can offer you more suggestions. Their website has good hiking details too. www.thehikehouse.com.

The book "Great Sedona Hikes" by William Bohan and David Butler is another good resource for great descriptions of local hikes and directions to the trailheads.

The National Forest Service covers the trails in detail along with maps. www.fs.usda.gov.

Where to Eat in Oak Creek Village

For dinner, we often had takeout and ate at our hotel room on our patio. The Village of Oak Creek has several restaurants close by. We tried to avoid going to uptown Sedona in the evenings. It's more touristy, and the traffic was usually overwhelming. Parking can be a challenge too.

Hilton rooms have a microwave and refrigerator so we purchased food at the grocery store and had light breakfast offerings and sandwich fixings to take on our outings for the day.

Grocery Store

Clark's Market is a full service grocery store within a 12 minute drive of the Hilton Sedona and located next to our favorite restaurant, Red Rock Cafe. It also has a terrific beer selection. 100 Verde Valley School Road.

Nearby Restaurants

Red Rock Cafe

Red Rock Cafe was our hands down favorite place to eat. Home of the giant cinnamon roll, it prides itself in serving a wonderful breakfast. They serve it all day, and it opens early at 7am and closes at 2pm.

We generally ate a light breakfast at home, packed snacks for a hike, and then stopped here on the way home. We also ordered the giant cinnamon roll (which feeds the entire family) to take home to enjoy at the hotel for breakfast the next morning.

Everything we tried was great! It's located a 12 minute drive from Hilton Sedona, which made it very convenient. 100 Verde Valley School Road.

Miley's Cafe

Also conveniently located near the Hilton Sedona (within a 10 minute walk), Miley's serves breakfast, lunch and dinner. We enjoyed tacos one night, but they offer a wide selection on their menu including burgers and salads. Kids menu as well.

Famous Pizza

This small restaurant is within a 5 minute drive of the Hilton Sedona and is located at 10 Bell Rock Plaza. Really good pizza! It has historically been voted Sedona's best pizza. Take out available. Another location can be found at 3190 West Highway 89A.

The Grill at Shadowrock (Hilton Sedona's Restaurant)

The hotel restaurant was average and a bit overpriced, but it offers lovely patio dining. Plus, at the time we were there, they offered a kids eat free with adult entree purchase.

Where to Eat in Sedona

Oak Creek Brewery offers pub food including fresh-made tamales and tasty beer. It's roughly 15 minutes north of Hilton Sedona, near the junction of 179/89. It's a good place to stop after hiking the trails in that area (Fay Canyon, Boynton Canyon, Devil's Bridge).

Cowboy Club is another good choice in uptown Sedona. It has a fun western decor and a nice outdoor patio. They serve a broad selection of appetizers, burgers, salads, etc. It's open for lunch and dinner and located a 15 minute drive from Hilton Sedona.

Day 5

Scenic Drive to Grand Canyon National Park--Eastern Entrance

Get an early start today. It's time to check out of your lodging and take a road trip to the Grand Canyon. Some people take a "day trip" to visit the Grand Canyon by way of the south entrance. If you can swing it though, We'd recommend at least one or two nights inside the national park entering through the east entrance with a few side stops on the way.

The Grand Canyon

If you choose to enter Grand Canyon National Park through its eastern entrance, you can make 4 really enjoyable stops:

1) **Oak Creek Canyon** to purchase Native American-made souvenirs
2) **Sunset Crater Volcano National Monument** to witness evidence of an extinct volcano
3) **The Wupatki National Monument** where you can walk through the pueblos that were occupied 900 years ago
4) **The Desert View Watch Tower** in Grand Canyon National Park for your first views of the Colorado River and the Grand Canyon

Stop 1- Oak Creek Canyon

It is a beautiful drive north on US 89 to the Grand Canyon and driving through Oak Creek Canyon from Sedona was a treat. There were several vendors at the Oak Creek Vista Overlook selling unique Native American crafts, pottery, and jewelry making it a great stop to take a break from the driving and stretch your legs. It's roughly 45 minutes from the Village of Oak Creek.

Forested Oak Creek Canyon- View from the overlook

Even if you don't include the Grand Canyon in your trip, you should considering the opportunity to visit Oak Creek Canyon during your stay in Sedona.

Stop 2- Sunset Crater Volcano National Monument

Just 40 minutes from Stop 1, you'll arrive at Sunset Crater Volcano National Monument. Allow 1 hour to stop at the Visitor Center and hike the one mile **Lava Flow Trail** to see the black, jagged and twisted lava and ash formed from extinct volcanoes. Self-guiding trail booklets are available for purchase in the Visitor Center.

A $20 vehicle fee covers entrance to both Sunset Crater and Wupatki National Monuments and admission is free with an America the Beautiful National Parks Pass. Sunset Crater is a little over one hour's drive from the Village of Oak Creek.

Lava Rock at Sunset Crater Volcano National Monument

Stop 3- Wupatki National Monument

If you have time for just one of these National Monuments, go here. The drive here is beautiful with views of the Painted Desert and the ponderosa highlands of northern Arizona in the distance. It's located just 25 minutes from Sunset Crater National Monument.

Stop at the Visitor Center and take a self-guided walk through the pueblos that were occupied 900 years ago. Visitors can even go inside the largest pueblo. Allow an hour.

From Wupatki National Monument, you will drive 1 hour and 10 minutes to the east entrance of the Grand Canyon.

Wupatki Indian Site

Stop 4- Grand Canyon National Park--Desert View Watch Tower

When entering from the east entrance, your first stop on the way to Canyon Village will be at the Desert View Watch Tower and Visitor Center. The tower is located 20 miles east of the park's Canyon Village where you will be staying, so now is a good time to visit it.

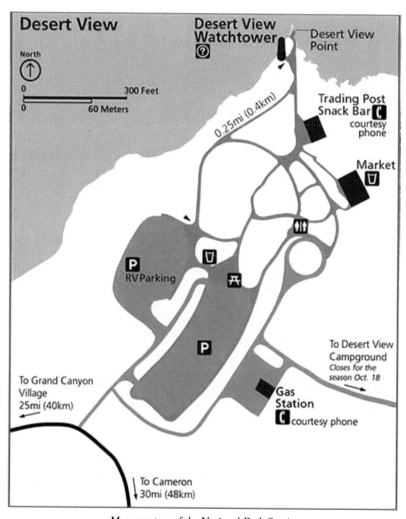

Map courtesy of the National Park Service

Some of the finest views of the Colorado River and canyon geology is seen from here. My girls loved climbing the stairs of the tower, and it was the perfect place for their first glimpse of the Grand Canyon.

Inside Desert View Watch Tower

Where to Stay at the Grand Canyon

If at all possible, stay inside the national park at one of their lodges or hotels. The lodging in the national park books quickly, so make your reservations well in advance. Take what you can get, but if you have a choice, book either the Kachina Lodge or El Tovar Hotel. They are located directly on the canyon rim and are nicely suited for families.

Tip: If you can't reserve your desired date, keep checking back on the website. You'll be surprised how quickly availability can change. If you can only get one night's lodging, go ahead and reserve it and check back frequently for the 2nd night. www.grandcanyonlodges.com

Kachina Lodge

We stayed at the Kachina Lodge with a partial canyon view room. It was very nice and clean and offered an excellent location. You can walk to trails and restaurants from this location and the rim of the canyon was right out the front door. It seemed like the best price point inside the park for its excellent canyon rim location.

Tip: Request a partial canyon view room on the second floor. All rooms come with a refrigerator too. Average rates: $240 per night canyon side; $225 night street side.

El Tovar Hotel

A historic hotel on the rim of the Grand Canyon. It is more expensive but beautiful. An excellent location within walking distance of trails and restaurants and the rim of the canyon is right outside. Starting at $263 night for 2 doubles and up to $538 for a suite.

Where to Eat at the Grand Canyon

El Tovar Hotel
Dining at historic national park lodges is a treat, so make reservations for dinner at the El Tovar Hotel. It's a good way to experience the hotel if you're not staying there. It's next door to Kachina Lodge.

Bright Angel Restaurant
Bright Angel Restaurant serves diner-style dishes for breakfast, lunch, and dinner. First come-first serve. No reservations needed.

Maswik Food Court
The food court will have something for everyone. It is located within Canyon Village, about a 15 minute walking distance from Kachina Lodge.

Activities at the Grand Canyon

Bike the South Rim

You can rent bicycles for the whole family from **Bright Angel Bicycles** inside the national park. Park at the Lot 4 parking area at the Grand Canyon Visitor Center. Their building is located directly off this lot. During the summer, they open as early as 7am and they remain open during the winter season (weather permitting). Check their website for current hours of operation: http://bikegrandcanyon.com/

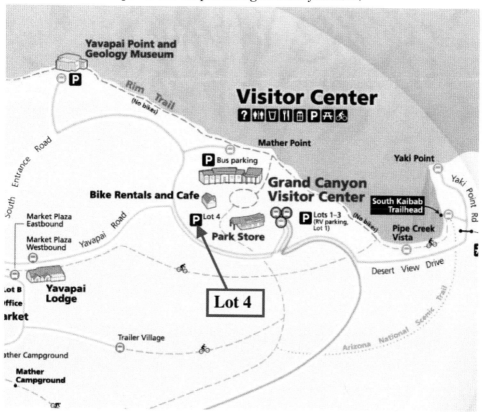

Bike Rentals in Grand Canyon Village- Map courtesy of the National Park Service

They offer bikes for both adults and children starting at $12 hour for adults/$9 for kids. **Tip:** Bike trailers and tag-alongs are also available for rent. Reservations are recommended, and you can make them online or give them a call.

Riders wanting an easy one-way 5 mile ride with 95% downhill or flat surfaces can shuttle to Hopi Point to ride from there to Hermits Rest on **Bright Angel Bike's "Red Bike Ride"** route. They also offer other "routes" as well. Check out their website for reservations and route descriptions to find one that best fits your family's needs. Keep in mind that the Grand Canyon sits at 7000' elevation, so high altitude fitness makes a difference here.

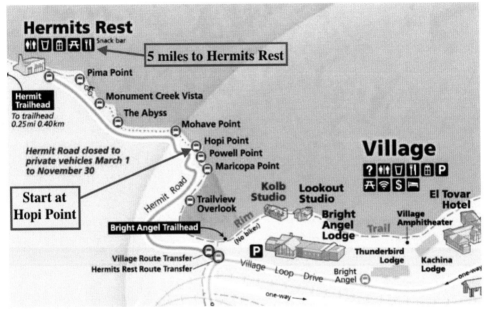

Shuttle to Hopi Point for an easy 5 mile ride to Hermits Rest- Map courtesy of the National Park Service

Walk the Rim Trail

The easy Rim Trail extends roughly 12 miles from the Village area near Kolb Studio to Hermits Rest. Begin from any viewpoint in the Village or along Hermit Road. The Rim Trail offers excellent walking for quiet views of the inner canyon. By using the free in-park shuttle buses, you can customize your hike to meet your needs (hike one way and shuttle back or shuttle to your start point). Or, just stroll along the section closest to your lodging and enjoy the views.

Bright Angel Trail

The Bright Angel Trail leads from the South Rim of the Grand Canyon down the canyon to the Colorado River. The trailhead is located just west of Bright Angel Lodge. **Note:** This is a strenuous 12 mile out and back hike and is not considered a day hike. With our kids, we simply walked about 20 minutes down the trail and then returned.

Realize that walking up is much, much harder than going down and the temperatures are rising every minute during the warmer seasons.

At the 1.5 mile marker the elevation has already changed 1000 feet. Here you will find a rest station with water and restrooms. We did not make it this far with our young kiddos, but even our short walk on the trail was beautiful and fascinating.

Tips: Hike in the morning before it's too hot, bring a camera, stick to a time limit, and bring enough drinking water. It is such a beautiful trail and experiencing it for even a short duration is memorable. My husband and I took turns later without the girls to hike further.

Bright Angel Trailhead

Attend a Ranger Program

Check out the schedule of Ranger Programs and make sure you attend one or two. The rangers are well spoken and make the topics interesting for the whole family. It really made us appreciate our experience even more. Kids can also become a Junior Ranger. Highly recommend this activity!

www.simplyawesometrips.com

That's all for this itinerary. Have a blast in Sedona and the Grand Canyon and make sure to drink plenty of water and apply sunscreen! Send us your best photo (#simplyawesometrips) and we will happily post it to our Instagram page. We love seeing vacation photos, honest!

To see more photos of the places mentioned in this guidebook- check out the album labeled "Sedona" on our Facebook page.

If you find an amazing restaurant, lodging, or activity that you think we should include in future editions or simply have a question or comment about anything in this itinerary, we would love to hear from you. Shoot us an email at: info@simplyawesometrips.com.

If you loved this guidebook, please take a moment to help fellow travelers find it by adding a review to our book listing on Amazon!

Happy Trails and Safe Travels!

Amy & Amanda

Additional Titles Available on Amazon and Our Website

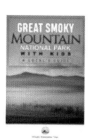

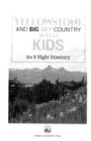
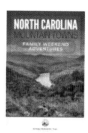

A Thank You Gift!

As a thank you for your purchase, we invite you to visit our website at www.simplyawesometrips.com to purchase a detailed trip itinerary to a destination of your choice for just $5. Use code SEDONA2019. The offer is good for one itinerary from our website only (pdf format) and expires at the end of 2019.

Our goal is to help you plan a fantastic trip for you and your family!

Disclosures and Liability Statement

Although the author has made every effort to ensure that the information in this itinerary was correct at the time of publishing, the author does not assume and hereby disclaims any liability to any party for any loss, damage, or disruption caused by errors or omissions, whether such errors or omissions result from negligence, accident, or any other cause. The authors, publishers, and contributors to this itinerary, either directly or indirectly, disclaim any liability for injuries, accidents, and damages, whatsoever that may occur to those using this guide. You are responsible for your health and safety for all aspects of this itinerary. Be safe and use good judgment.

By providing links to other sites, Simply Awesome Trips does not guarantee, approve, or endorse, the information or products available on these sites.

All maps courtesy of OpenStreetMap www.openstreetmap.org/copyright unless otherwise noted.

Made in the USA
Columbia, SC
19 December 2019